JOHN MUIR

by Sally Tolan

For a free color catalog describing Gareth Stevens' list of high-quality children's books, call 1-800-341-3569.

Picture Credits

American Academy and Institute of Arts and Letters — 38; American Geographical Society Collection, University of Wisconsin-Milwaukee Library — 30, 51; Bancroft Library, University of California-Berkeley — 49, 52, 54; Corcoran Gallery of Art — 19; DeWalt and Associates — © Rick Karpinski, cover; © Gareth Stevens, Inc., maps by Sharon Burris — 22, 40, 60; Greenpeace — © S. Kittner, 57; © Matthew Groshek — 44; Lake County (Illinois) Museum, Curt Teich Postcard Collection — 6, 37, 46 (both); Milwaukee County Historical Society — 10, 18; Muir-Hanna Trust — 4, 11, 16 (both), 27, 29, 32, 35, 41; National Aeronautics and Space Administration — 58; © The Nature Conservancy — photograph by Susan Bournique, 42; Oakland Museum — 28, 33; Collection of the State Historical Society of Wisconsin: 13, 14 (photograph by Deborah Grossfield, Madison Art Center), 20, 59; Tom Stack and Associates — © Larry Lipski, 48: Milton Rand, 12: © Spencer Swanger, 8; United States Department of Agriculture, Forest Service — 55; United States Department of the Interior, National Park Service, Yosemite National Park — 26, 36; United States Geological Survey, W. B. Hamilton — 23; University of Wisconsin-Madison Archives — 17.

A Gareth Stevens Children's Books edition

Edited, designed, and produced by
Gareth Stevens Children's Books
RiverCenter Building, Suite 201
1555 North RiverCenter Drive
Milwaukee, Wisconsin 53212, USA

Library of Congress Cataloging-in-Publication Data

Tolan, Sally.
     John Muir / by Sally Tolan.
          p. cm. — (People who have helped the world)
     Includes index.
     Summary: A biography of the naturalist who, among other activities, founded the Sierra Club and, as an early proponent of wilderness preservation, was influential in establishing the national park system.
     ISBN 0-8368-0099-0
     1. Muir, John, 1838-1914—Juvenile literature. 2. Conservationists—United States—Biography—Juvenile literature. 3. Naturalists—United States—Biography—Juvenile literature. [1. Muir, John, 1838-1914. 2. Naturalists. 3. Conservationists.] I. Title. II. Series.
     QH31.M9T65   1989   333.7'2'0924—dc19   [B]   [92]   89-4367

Series conceived by Helen Exley
Series editor: Rhoda Irene Sherwood
Research editor: Scott Enk
Picture editor: Matthew Groshek
Layout: Kristi Ludwig

Printed in the United States of America

1 2 3 4 5 6 7 8 9 96 95 94 93 92 91 90

JOHN MUIR

Naturalist, writer, and guardian of the North American wilderness

by Sally Tolan

Gareth Stevens Children's Books
MILWAUKEE

A new beginning

On a March morning in 1868, John Muir arrived by ship in San Francisco. Behind him, he had left his parents, brothers and sisters, friends, and a chance for success and riches. Now, as he hurried through the bustling streets of San Francisco, he asked a passerby the fastest way out of town. The man inquired of Muir where he wanted to go. "Anywhere," Muir replied, "that is wild."

Actually, John Muir knew where he wanted to go. He had heard and read about a valley called Yosemite, with its splendid rock walls and surrounding mountains. And that is where he headed. He did not know then that Yosemite would be his home, his classroom, and his laboratory for years. He did not know that he would become its most famous defender. Nor could he imagine that he would some day influence presidents and congressmen to save Yosemite and other wilderness lands from destruction by creating national parks and forests.

During his life of advocacy for nature, he would continue to study and explore nature. He would study rocks for clues to the land's history, climb mountains, tour the forests of the West, clamber over Alaskan glaciers. He would become an expert on plants, glaciers, rocks, and on the interconnections among all parts of creation. Through his writing, he would share his knowledge and passionate love of nature with readers across the country. Many of these readers themselves would become advocates for nature and support his efforts to preserve the wilderness.

Like the prophet, John the Baptist, Muir would, in the early years, be a "voice of one crying in the wilderness." He would raise his voice on behalf of the wilderness and against the forces of destruction. He would fight against greedy and wasteful lumbering

Opposite: Muir in his student days at the University of Wisconsin in Madison, 1863. He trimmed his beard and hair and put on his best suit for this photograph, his first. Because his father did not approve of having pictures in the house, none of the family members had been photographed before then. But after they saw John's photo, his mother and brothers and sisters all had their pictures taken. John's father did not.

"Part of Muir's attractiveness to modern readers is the fact that he was an activist. He not only explored the west and wrote about its beauties — he fought for their preservation. His successes dot the landscape in all the natural features that bear his name: forests, lakes, trails, glaciers. His writings still stimulate readers to try to retrace his footsteps through areas about which he wrote so compellingly."

Frank E. Buske, from the introduction to John Muir's Wilderness Essays

The U.S. government has expanded the national park system to include areas with unique geological features. This postcard shows an active volcano in Hawaii National Park, as depicted in the 1920s.

practices, ruinous livestock grazing on fragile lands, needless flooding of a priceless valley. He would not win all of his battles, but he would awaken a nation to its precious natural heritage. He and his allies would found the Sierra Club, an organization that would carry on his fight for the wilderness long after Muir had died.

But on that spring morning in 1868, he merely knew that he wanted to live close to nature. He had recently hiked and camped through Wisconsin, Indiana, and Ontario, Canada. He had embarked on a 1,000-mile walk (1,600 km) across the southeastern United States. And always, he had observed, taken notes, and drawn conclusions about the wonders of the land. Now, at nearly thirty, he was ready for the mountains and valleys of California.

The Muirs in Scotland

John Muir was born in Dunbar, Scotland, on April 21, 1838. He had two older sisters, Margaret and Sarah, two younger brothers, David and Daniel, Jr., and twin sisters, Mary and Annie. All were born in Dunbar. Another sister, Joanna, was born after the family moved to the United States.

John's father, Daniel Muir, was a man of strong feelings. When John was a young boy, his father sometimes played the fiddle and joined the children and his wife in singing and laughter. But as the years passed, he became more stern. His religious beliefs made him put aside fun and music. Mealtime was a sacrament, he said, and there would be no idle talk or laughing at the table. John had to memorize a passage of the Bible every day. If he could not recite it correctly, his father beat him.

Of course John resented his father's harsh treatment, but he learned his Bible lessons. In his youth, he believed firmly in his father's vision of God and morality; in later years, however, he would reject his father's religious views. But Muir resembled his father in one way: he would one day cherish, with all the passion of his father, a new religion — a belief in the sacredness of all life.

John's mother, Ann Gilrye Muir, was a gentle, kind woman. She had been brought up to appreciate poetry and art. When she told her parents she wanted to marry Daniel Muir, her parents had resisted. They did not want her to marry him because they considered him too strict and passionate in his religious views. But Ann was strong-willed and she loved Daniel. Later she would find it hard to have a husband who believed that fun was the devil's workshop, a husband who would allow no pictures on the wall because he had read in the Bible a prohibition against "graven images."

She would find it hard, too, to leave her parents and friends in Dunbar to move across the sea to America. In those days, however, a husband was considered the ruler of the home, and his wife, as a rule, felt compelled to obey him. From this gentle and patient woman, John may have learned his love of beauty and his compassion for others.

In Scotland, Muir's schoolmasters were as harsh in their discipline as his father. Students who did not know their lessons or who got into fights in the school yard would feel the sting of the teacher's switch. John was a bright student, and had a keen memory, but he was also mischievous and had his share of whippings at school as well as at home.

The rolling hills of Scotland. Muir loved those times when he could explore the land, whether with his brother Daniel or his grandfather.

"When I was a boy in Scotland I was fond of everything that was wild, and all my life I've been growing fonder and fonder of wild places and wild creatures."

John Muir, in The Story of My Boyhood and Youth

Escape into nature

But John found some escape. His parents had a beautiful garden where the children often played. As John and David grew, though, they were not willing to stay home and play as their father ordered. Often they would climb over the wall and run out with their friends into the countryside or to the nearby seashore. They climbed on the rocky ruins of an old Scottish castle and clambered over farm walls, looking for birds' nests or apples from a farmer's orchard.

The boys' grandparents also offered them chances to escape the strict limits set by their father. Grandfather and Grandmother Gilrye lived just across the street from the Muirs, and the children often visited them. When John was a little boy, his grandfather would take him for walks in the countryside near their town. Once when they were sitting on a haystack in a field, John heard a "sharp, prickly, stinging cry." When he dug into the hay to find out what was making the cry, he found a mother field mouse with six baby mice. He was full of wonder at this sight, as he would often be in natural settings. Even after years of wilderness experience, animal life would always seem miraculous to him.

A new land

The life of the Muir family in Scotland would soon change, however. Daniel Muir had become unhappy with the Presbyterian church of his wife's family. So he had joined the Disciples of Christ.

Some of his fellow Disciples had begun to form religious communities in North America. There, Daniel heard, they had found rich farmland and a chance for success that was not possible in the cramped economy of Scotland.

On the evening of February 18, 1849, John and David were sitting at their grandparents' fireside doing schoolwork. Suddenly, their father rushed in. "Bairns," he said, "you needna learn your lessons the nicht, for we're gan to America the morn!"

America! At last. John had read of this land of forests, sugar maple trees and wild birds, gold and freedom. No more strict schoolmasters and hard grammar lessons. The boys were crazy with excitement. But Grandfather solemnly said, "Ah, poor laddies, poor laddies, you'll find something else ower the sea forbye gold and sugar, birds' nests and freedom fra lessons and schools. You'll find plenty hard, hard work."

Hard work in the New World

Grandfather was right. After a journey of a few months, the family settled in Marquette County, Wisconsin. Although John and his brothers and sisters loved the woods and lakes of their new home, they had little time to enjoy them. It was not unusual in those times for children to work long hours on family farms. But even the Muirs' neighbors noticed how hard Daniel Muir worked his children.

Daniel had become a preacher and a strict and harsh parent who believed that when he whipped his children, he was beating the devil out of their souls. While John and his brothers and sisters and a few hired men planted and hoed, raked and harvested, Daniel spent less and less time on farm work and more time studying his Bible or riding off to preach at small churches in neighboring settlements.

When their father was away, John and his brothers and sisters could joke and sing. The girls could bring

"There is one thing I hate with a perfect hatred — cruelty for anything or anybody."

John Muir, quoted in Linnie Marsh Wolfe's Son of the Wilderness: The Life of John Muir

9

In the era before tractors, horses or oxen pulled farm wagons and plows. Farms were smaller then than they are today when powerful tractors can cover many more acres each day than farm animals could.

"When we first saw Fountain Lake, on a sultry evening, sprinkled with millions of lightening bugs throbbing with light, the effect was so strange and beautiful that it seemed too marvelous to be real."
    John Muir, *in* The Story of My Boyhood and Youth

out their embroidery, which they had hidden from their father because he considered it frivolous. Their mother would join in the fun, laughing as John, the family clown, recited a silly poem or danced a highland jig.

As the oldest son, John had the hardest work: splitting rails for fences, prying up rocks, hauling wood. He had just turned twelve and his head barely reached the plow handles when his father set him to plowing the farm's first fields. The ground had never been broken, so John had to dig out tree roots and guide the plow as the oxen pulled it through tough, matted ground.

The Muirs grew wheat and corn on this farm, crops earning good prices. But after eight years, these drained nutrients out of the soil. Farmers knew little then about maintaining fertile soil. And they didn't worry because there was plenty of new land nearby. So when Fountain Lake was no longer fertile, the Muirs moved to a place they called Hickory Hill. Again, John labored in the fields clearing new land for crops. It was hard work for a boy and took its toll on John's health. But in more than ten years of farm work, he learned endurance and developed strength.

Overcoming fear

That strength and endurance carried John through struggles when he became an adult — and on one occasion, helped him when he was still a young boy. On the Muirs' first Wisconsin farm, surrounded by woods, was the small lake the family called Fountain Lake. Here, after the children had completed their farm chores, Daniel Muir encouraged them to teach themselves to swim.

One day John, David, and a friend were down at the lake. Their friend was fishing in deep water from the family's homemade rowboat. John decided to swim out to his friend. When he reached the boat, he raised his arm to grab hold. But he slipped, sank, and nearly panicked and drowned. Somehow he managed to kick himself to shallower water and was pulled into the rowboat by his friend.

John was so ashamed of his fear and failure that the next day he rowed himself out to the deepest part of the lake, and dove in and pushed himself up again and again. Each time he dove, he scolded himself, "Take that!" Never again did John Muir lose control of himself in the water — or in other dangerous situations in the wild.

The Hickory Hill farm-house, so named because it sat on a hill near a grove of hickory trees. John nearly died here when digging a well. One day, after being lowered by bucket 80 feet (24 m) into the well, he was overcome by carbonic acid gas that had accumulated at the bottom during the night. Daniel rescued him that day, and every morning after that they cleared the well by pouring in water and then lowering and raising brush or hay to lift out the gas and bring down fresh air.

11

A water ouzel. This little bird flits and dives in the spray of the waterfalls of Yosemite, and builds its nests in nearby rocks. Muir described the ouzel's song as "sweet and fluty" and its nature as "cheerful and calm."

"Of the many advantages of farm life . . . one of the greatest is . . . gaining a real knowledge of animals as fellow-mortals, learning to respect them and love them, and even to win some of their love. Thus godlike sympathy grows and thrives and spreads far beyond the teachings of churches and schools, where too often the mean, blinding, loveless doctrine is taught that animals have neither mind nor soul, have no rights that we are bound to respect, and were made only for man, to be petted, spoiled, slaughtered, or enslaved."

John Muir, in The Story of My Boyhood and Youth

Respect for animals

During these years, Muir learned to respect and love the creatures of the woods and farm. In *The Story of My Boyhood and Youth*, he describes his joy in the wild birds of the Wisconsin fields and woodlands: the little black-capped chickadees who stayed all winter, the fat, red-breasted robins, the wild ducks nesting at the lake, the now extinct passenger pigeon, and perhaps his favorite singer, the "little speckle-breasted song sparrow."

The woods were full of animals, too: deer, squirrels, woodchucks, muskrats, foxes, badgers, and even bears. John and David hunted as boys, but in later years, John stopped what he came to call "all this bloody flesh and sport business."

On the farm the Muirs had cats and dogs, horses, cows, and oxen. The boys rode their pony, Jack, bareback and pell-mell, across fields and hollows. Muir called Jack "the stoutest, gentlest, bravest little horse I ever saw." He saw the cows' devotion to their calves and the patience and intelligence of the oxen.

One night, when John's father was coming home from a religious meeting, he tried to steer his two oxen onto a shortcut off the trail. Suddenly the oxen stopped and refused to go on. Finally, Daniel Muir unhitched the two, grabbed hold of the tail of one, and let them lead him home in the dark.

When he went back for the wagon the next morning, he saw that the oxen had stopped at the top of a hill, just above an impassable swamp. John would remember this incident. For him, it served as an illustration of the intelligence of so-called "dumb" animals. Often, in later years, he would find reason to marvel at the good sense of wild animals and enjoy a feeling of kinship with them.

A budding inventor

John and his brothers and sisters did not go to school during those years of farm work. But he borrowed books from neighbors who kept a small library and read them in spare moments.

His father saw no reason to read anything except the Bible and other religious texts. So he wouldn't allow John to stay up and read after the others had

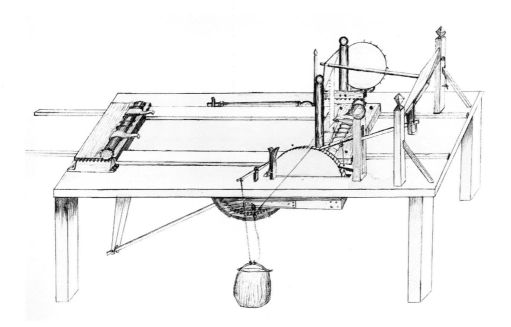

A table saw, drawn by Muir around 1860. This device, like most of his inventions, could save time and effort for workers. Although Daniel Muir thought that inventing was a waste of time, John's employers appreciated and profited by his inventive genius.

gone to bed. He did say, though, that John could get up early to read. And John did, often at 1:00 A.M.

In winter it was too cold to sit still and read, and Muir knew his father would not let him put extra wood in the heating stove. So he began working in the cellar on ideas for labor-saving machines. His first invention was a model of a sawmill. Soon he had also invented and built waterwheels, thermometers, clocks, a device for lighting fires and lamps, and an "early-or-late-rising machine." This device was made up of a clock attached to a bed. At a preset hour, the clock would somehow tip the bed on end and dump the startled sleeper out on his feet!

John's inventions became famous in the neighborhood. Some people thought they were freakish things and that John was strange. But a neighbor encouraged John to take his inventions to Madison, Wisconsin's capital, where he could exhibit them at the state's agricultural fair. When John wondered aloud if they would be interesting to people there, the neighbor insisted, "There's nothing else like them in the world. That is what will attract attention, and besides they're mighty handsome things anyway to come from the backwoods."

"He was a real live inventive, designing mechanic, systematic, practical; and it was a delight to see those machines at work."
William Trout, quoted in
Linnie Marsh Wolfe's
Son of the Wilderness:
The Life of John Muir

Leaving home

It was 1860. John was 22 years old and not sure what he wanted to do. Many summer nights he walked in the woods and fields of Marquette County, enjoying the soft summer air and starry skies but wondering if he should leave the farm.

Although he was tired of his father's strict and narrow rule, he loved the rest of his family deeply. But he was beginning to realize how much he wanted to study science and to travel throughout the world. So he decided to take an exhibit to Madison and see where this might lead him.

At the fair, people crowded around John's exhibit. His inventions were a hit and were written about in the local newspaper. People called him a genius. Back home, his mother and sisters and brothers were proud of and happy for him. But his father, who had refused to say goodbye when John left the farm, wrote him sternly, warning him to avoid the "sin of vanity."

A new friend

At the fair, John Muir met a woman who would become a great friend and helper in his life. Her name was Jeanne Carr.

Mrs. Carr was impressed by the inventive farm youth. She herself was well educated and perhaps as fascinated with the world of nature as Muir was. For many years she would encourage John in his studies of nature and, later, in his writing career.

Her husband, Dr. Ezra Carr, was a professor of natural science at the university, with a special interest in geology. In early 1861, after he decided to enroll at the university, John would become one of Dr. Carr's students. He would also become a friend of the family and sometimes take care of the Carr children. Through the Carrs, Muir was introduced to many of the great thinkers and scientists of the day, both in person and through the books in the Carrs' library.

Muir did not immediately enroll at the university because of concern about money. Instead, he helped build iceboats, addressed advertising circulars, and drove a coach for an insurance agent. But one day, on the university's campus, he learned during a chat with a student that he could, indeed, afford to attend.

Opposite: Muir's room at the university was full of his inventions. This one is a desk with a built-in clock and gears that moved a book to the front for him to study and after fifteen minutes moved another book up to take its place. This desk is now at the State Historical Society of Wisconsin in Madison.

"I have often in my heart wondered what God was training you for. He gave you the eye within the eye, to see in all natural objects the realized ideas of His mind. He gave you pure tastes, and the sturdy preference of whatsoever is most lovely and excellent. He has made you a more individualized existence than is common, and by your very nature, removed you from common temptations. . . . He will surely place you where your work is."

Letter to Muir from Jeanne Carr, quoted in Linnie Marsh Wolfe's Son of the Wilderness: The Life of John Muir

Ezra S. Carr, professor of chemistry and geology.

Jeanne C. Carr, an important supporter of Muir's from his early twenties until he married at forty-two. The Carrs were active in the National Grange, an organization of people working to protect farmers from exploitation by business. She helped her husband with his work and frequently lectured on topics like women's rights.

University days: hard times but inspiring teachers

John Muir could manage at the university by eating simple meals, renting a cheap room, and spending little on clothing. In those days, men's fashions included stiff collars, fancy vests and suit coats, and neatly trimmed hair and beards.

It was fortunate that these were not John's style, for he could not have afforded to keep up with fashion. With only about fifty cents to spend on food each week, he lived on graham crackers and water.

One day, John's family learned from a friend who had visited him in Madison that John was near collapse because he could afford only crackers to eat. Daniel Muir's conscience finally prodded him to send John some money.

The next year at the university, John had a teaching job in a one-room school a few miles outside of Madison. It was hard to keep up with his teaching and his own studies, but because of the money he earned by teaching, his diet improved considerably.

Yet these years were fulfilling to John. He later wrote that the university seemed to him to be "next to the Kingdom of Heaven." The hard times were the price John paid for what he saw as a great opportunity. He took chemistry and geology classes from Dr. Carr and Latin and Greek classes from Dr. James Davie Butler. Both men opened new worlds for John.

Dr. Carr had studied with some of the world's leading natural scientists, including Louis Agassiz, the great Swiss geologist, who taught at Harvard University in Massachusetts. Agassiz's studies of glaciers led him to believe that they played a major role in shaping landforms.

These views were both influential and controversial. Dr. Carr and many leading scientists respected Agassiz's theory that a great Ice Age had shaped much of the Earth's landscape.

But other people believed that these marks on the landscape were the result of Noah's flood or some other catastrophe. They wanted scientific theory to fit the familiar stories of the Bible. While at the university, John became fascinated with the ideas of Agassiz and Dr. Carr, and only a few years later he

UNIVERSITY, MADISON, WIS.

would make his own important studies of glaciers as he lived and traveled in western North America.

From Dr. Butler, John learned to observe carefully and to write. Dr. Butler urged his students to write in a natural tone and to include small details.

John also learned from Dr. Butler the importance of keeping a "commonplace book" or journal. In his later travels and throughout his years of studying nature, John almost always had a small notebook in which he recorded his observations and thoughts. From those jottings and the many letters he wrote to close friends came most of the articles and books he would later write.

In his second year at the university, John became fascinated with botany. He often went into the woods and fields botanizing — collecting plants and studying them. At the time he didn't realize how lasting this interest would be.

For the rest of his life, throughout his years of studying other parts of nature, he would continue the study of plants, even as he examined other features of nature. In fact, in the years ahead he would discover many unknown types of plants — and even have some named for him.

A view of the University of Wisconsin campus in 1868. Between 1861 and 1863, when Muir attended, it had fewer than 200 students. While here, Muir was able to pursue his studies exclusively, without the distraction of farm labor.

"I shall not forget the Doctor, who first laid before me the great book of nature."

John Muir, speaking of Ezra Carr, quoted in Linnie Marsh Wolfe's Son of the Wilderness: The Life of John Muir

17

Civil war — and indecision

During John's college years, the United States was suffering through the Civil War. Many university students joined the army and went off in high spirits to what they expected to be a great patriotic adventure. But John did not share their enthusiasm for war. He saw the pain of the sick and wounded as they came back from the war and wanted to help these men. So he decided to go to medical school at the University of Michigan after finishing at Wisconsin.

But John's plans changed. He was not sure what he should do, but he knew that he loved the study of nature and must continue it. And he feared that he would be drafted into the army whether he stayed in Wisconsin or went to Michigan for medical school. He did not want to fight in the war because he did not approve of killing and because he did not want to risk his life in war. He still felt more a Scotsman than an American and felt no desire to fight in a war for his adopted country.

In August of 1863, when John was 25, he went home and lived and worked through the fall and winter on the farm of his sister Sarah and her husband, David Galloway. During this period, he came to a decision — he would not yet go to medical school. Nor would he settle down and start a profession, as his friends and family urged. Instead, he would go botanizing in Canada at the first sign of spring. His brother Daniel had already gone to Canada to avoid being drafted, and John planned to meet him near Niagara Falls in September.

"The University of the Wilderness"

On March 1, 1864, he caught a train in nearby Portage, Wisconsin, and headed north. He tramped through northern Michigan and crossed into Canada, exploring the woods and marshes of southern Ontario along Lake Huron's Georgian Bay.

He met Dan at Niagara Falls, and for the next few months, they lived and worked in Meaford, Ontario. When the Civil War ended in 1865, Dan went on to Buffalo, New York, and John moved on to Indianapolis, Indiana, partially so that he could be near the vast forests outside the city.

John had left the University of Wisconsin, but his education was not completed. As he later wrote, he realized he was about to enter "the University of the Wilderness." In the four years he worked in Meaford and Indianapolis, he was able to drift between his beloved wilderness and jobs in which he applied his inventive skills. In fact, this would be a lifelong pattern. For the rest of his years, the wilderness would

"I left the University without the slightest thought of making a name, but urged on and on in search of beauty and knowledge. Away I wandered happy and free and poor into the glorious American wilderness."
John Muir, quoted in John Muir: To Yosemite and Beyond, *edited by Robert Engberg and Donald Wesling*

Niagara Falls, in a painting by Frederick Church. In 1864, John and Daniel camped near the falls before going on to work at a sawmill and factory in Meaford, Ontario.

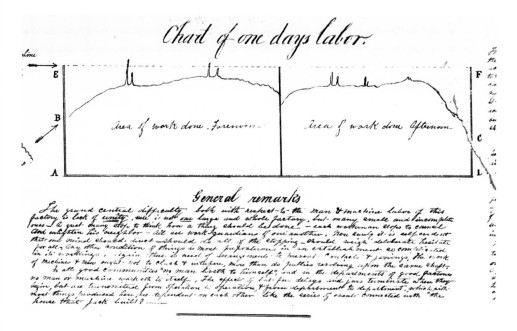

Chart of one days labor.

Area of work done. Forenoon.   *Area of work done Afternoon.*

General remarks

A page from one of Muir's efficiency studies done for Osgood, Smith & Co., which made carriage wheels in Indianapolis. One of his recommendations was to reduce the workday from ten to eight hours because productivity dropped and the number of accidents rose during the last two hours of a ten-hour workday.

call him from home and family and work. And always it would restore and inspire him.

During this period, John realized that although he loved being out in the midst of nature and enjoyed the challenges of his jobs, he sometimes felt lonely. So he welcomed Jeanne Carr's suggestion that they write letters to one another and share their thoughts and observations. Jeanne Carr appreciated John's love of nature and enjoyed hearing about his adventures and dreams. She herself was a lifelong student of botany, so they often wrote about the wild plants John encountered. In her letters she gave him both encouragement and friendship that helped him through many lonely hours. Their correspondence was to last ten years.

The inventor at work

While in Meaford and Indianapolis, Muir proved to be as adept a worker as he was a student of nature. In Ontario, he had worked with his brother Dan at Trout & Jay, a sawmill and rake company. In Indianapolis, he worked for a company that manufactured carriage parts. In both jobs, his inventions increased production and saved money for his employers. In the Indianapolis position, he also began studying the hours and patterns of work in the factory and recommending changes to make the plant operate more efficiently. As one of the nation's earliest efficiency experts, he could have been a leader in an important and expanding field. His special gift was that he could recognize the interconnectedness of workers, departments, and the whole organization, just as he would come to see the interrelationships in nature. He might have had a permanent career in industry, but fate intervened.

A turning point

A serious accident changed John's plans. One day in the plant in Indianapolis, he was using a file to tighten a machine belt. The file flew out of his hand and the sharp end pierced his right eye. His left eye, in reaction, also dimmed. He was desperate, fearing he would never see his wilderness world again.

In Meaford and Indianapolis, John had become engrossed in working on his inventions. He had had little time for exploring the mysteries of nature, except on weekends, when he took groups of nature students out into the woods. He had made friends with his students and their families, as he had with his employers and fellow workers.

Now the help and affection of those friends was to be crucial! Some friends brought an eye specialist to see John. Others read to him. Children brought him flowers and listened to his stories.

Finally, after days in a darkened room, John felt his sight begin to return. His bosses, grateful for the work he'd done for their company, offered him a foreman's job and a future partnership. But John had realized something during his period of blindness. He would give up the chance for wealth and success in industry. He would not waste his God-given sight on machines but instead would use his eyes to see and study the beauties of creation.

And now it was time to begin. He would go off on a three-year journey, immersing himself in the wilderness. Then he would decide about settling down. Years later he would write, "I might have become a millionaire, but I chose to become a tramp!"

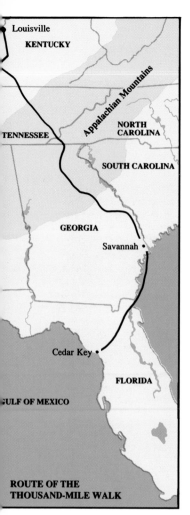

Louisville
KENTUCKY

TENNESSEE

Appalachian Mountains

NORTH CAROLINA

SOUTH CAROLINA

GEORGIA

Savannah •

Cedar Key •

FLORIDA

;ULF OF MEXICO

**ROUTE OF THE
THOUSAND-MILE WALK**

So John said goodbye to his friends in Indianapolis. After a visit to Wisconsin to see his family, he was ready to become immersed in the study of nature. But he would not work in a laboratory and peer through a microscope. Instead, he would enter nature's world — he would walk through her woods, climb her hills and mountains, and live among her trees and rocks.

The thousand-mile walk

On September 1, 1867, John stepped off a train in Louisville, Kentucky. The next day, carrying only his plant press, a few clothes and books, and some bread and tea, he set out on foot to walk from Louisville to Florida, a distance of 1,000 miles (1,600 km). In Florida, he planned to catch a boat for South America. He was eager to see the plants of southern lands.

He walked along the most deserted and wild paths. As he went, he stopped to collect plant samples and write about his observations in his journal. On the first page he wrote, "John Muir, Earth-Planet, Universe." He envisioned himself as a citizen of not just one town or nation, but of all creation.

Along the way, Muir slept outside or in the cabins of country people with whom he sometimes had supper. As he traveled, he marveled at his first sight of mountains; the Midwest had not prepared him for the Cumberland Mountains of Tennessee. And in Georgia, he was taken with the great live oak trees draped with Spanish moss. In Savannah, he took a boat to the northeast coast of Florida and in eight days hiked across northern Florida. Palmettos, mangroves, other subtropical plants, alligators in the swamps — all fascinated him.

Muir arrived in a small settlement on the Gulf Coast of Florida, on October 23, fifty-three days after he had left Louisville. In a few days he collapsed with a terrible fever, probably due to malaria. As he had during recovery from his eye injury, Muir spent much of this period of illness thinking about the direction of his life. His notes in his journal show that by this time he had rejected the narrow religious views of his father. He had adopted a set of spiritual beliefs that placed high value on the plant and animal world, as well as the human. He now saw all parts of creation as valuable in themselves, not just for what they could provide to humans. In addition to reverence for God and man, he had reverence for nature.

To California

In January 1868, still weak from his illness, John decided that this was not the time for him to explore the Amazon in South America. He would need a great deal of strength for such a strenuous trip. Having heard about the beauty of Yosemite Valley in California, he decided to go there instead.

To get to California, he would have to cross the Isthmus of Panama. (The Panama Canal was not yet built.) But he could not find a ship that was heading directly to Panama, so he took a ship to New York, then another to Panama, and, after crossing Panama by train, another to San Francisco. Then, with a shipmate who was looking for work in California, he arrived in San Francisco in late March and immediately set off for the Yosemite Valley.

As the two men hiked east through vast meadows carpeted with golden and purple wildflowers, they saw the great Sierra Nevada mountain range. John

The Sierra Nevada mountain range. The Sierra Nevada extends along the eastern part of California, from the Cascade Range in the northern part of the state, over four hundred miles (640 km), to the Mojave Desert in the south. It covers about twenty percent of California. The name of the range comes from the Spanish sierra, *meaning "saw," and* nevada, *meaning "snow-covered."*

called it the "Range of Light" because of the brightness of the sunlit, snowy summits.

The Sierra Nevada range is full of canyons and valleys that were carved by ancient glaciers and that now shelter rivers and streams. The Yosemite Valley, 4,000 feet above sea level (6,400 km), is the most famous of these valleys. John Muir, in his book, *The Yosemite*, describes it this way:

"The walls are made up of rocks, mountains in size, partly separated from each other by side canyons, and they are so sheer in front, and so compactly and harmoniously arranged on a level floor, that the Valley, comprehensively seen, looks like an immense hall or temple lighted from above. . . . Down through the middle of the Valley flows the crystal Merced, River of Mercy, peacefully quiet, reflecting lilies and trees and the onlooking rocks. . . ."

When they came into the Yosemite Valley with its domes, rock walls, and waterfalls, they had walked more than one hundred miles (160 km). John was awed by the immensities. They stayed in the valley ten days and on the way out camped in the Merced Grove of huge sequoia trees. Again he was awestruck and determined to return.

He would have liked to go up into the mountains right then, but he needed to earn money for supplies and to have a reserve in case his family should need help. So for several months, he worked a few miles from Yosemite on farms and ranches in the San Joaquin Valley, taming wild horses and harvesting, shearing, and tending sheep.

Herding and exploring the Yosemite

While Muir may have felt this was time wasted, those months as a shepherd enabled him to explore the Sierra Nevada highlands above Yosemite Valley. There, he studied more closely the relationship of plants and animals to their environment.

He also began a careful study of landforms. Quite early, he learned about the damage the grazing sheep were doing to the mountain environment. In the summer of 1869, a sheep rancher asked Muir to supervise the move of his sheep up into the mountains where there were good summer pastures. This offer gave Muir a chance he'd been hoping for. A shepherd named Billy would do most of the work, and John would have time to explore the mountains.

That summer Muir came to know the rocks and plants and waterfalls of the Yosemite heights. He discovered marks on the rocks that convinced him that glaciers had carved out the canyons and valleys of Yosemite. He climbed out on an overhanging ledge so that he could look into the heart of a waterfall. He peered through his magnifying lens at mountain plants. He recorded his observations in both words and sketches in his journal.

He also wrote letters about what he saw and thought of this mountain world to his family and friends, especially Jeanne Carr, who had moved with her husband and children to Oakland, California, near San Francisco.

As the two men took the sheep to the beautiful meadows near the Tuolumne River, Muir became aware that the sheep were permanently harming the area's vegetation. He hated the way they destroyed the grasses and wildflowers. He later wrote, "To let sheep trample so divinely fine a place seems barbarous!"

While they camped for a month beside the Tuolumne River, Muir climbed mountain peaks, including Mount Dana and Mount Lyell, both over 13,000 feet high (3,900 m). He also hiked through canyons. There, he found even more evidence of the workings of glaciers, more support for his beliefs.

As he explored and studied he became more and more convinced that nature is "one living, pulsing organism." Just as he had seen the interconnections between the workers, machines, and departments at the factory in Indianapolis, he now was seeing more clearly the relationship between rocks, soil, water, plants, and animals — including humans.

Becoming a guide to the Yosemite

Muir would continue to be a student in the University of the Wilderness all his life. And now he was about to become a teacher too, as he had been briefly in Meaford and Indianapolis. He had wanted to know Yosemite Valley in all its seasons. In order to spend

"More wild knowledge, less arithmetic and grammar — compulsory education in the form of woodcraft, mountain craft, science at first hand."

John Muir describing the ideal schooling, quoted in John Muir: To Yosemite and Beyond, edited by Robert Engberg and Donald Wesling

"Walk away quietly in any direction and taste the freedom of the mountaineer. Camp out among the grasses and gentians of glacial meadows, in craggy garden nooks full of Nature's darlings. Climb the mountains and get their good tidings. Nature's peace will flow into you as sunshine flows into trees. The winds will blow their own freshness into you, and the storms their energies, while cares will drop off like autumn leaves."

John Muir, quoted in Shirley Sargent's John Muir in Yosemite

the winter there, he got a job as a sawyer for J. M. Hutchings, who owned and operated a hotel in the valley. As Muir spent more time there he came to know the Yosemite more intimately.

In the spring Hutchings was away. One of Muir's jobs was to lead guided tours through the area. In Hutchings' absence, Muir took over and began guiding tourists who wanted to explore the valley. Many of the tourists were impressed by Muir's knowledge of Yosemite and by his enthusiastic love of nature. Jeanne Carr, who was keeping in touch with Muir through their continuing correspondence, began to tell visitors to ask for him as a guide.

In May of 1871 Muir served as a guide for a man whose writings on man and nature had long inspired him — Ralph Waldo Emerson, the famous writer and philosopher from Concord, Massachusetts, and a friend of the Carrs. He had heard about Muir from Jeanne Carr. And Muir had read Emerson's essays about nature and self-reliance and deeply respected the great old man. He shared Emerson's belief that humans are most noble when they are close to nature and when they rely on their own resources.

Emerson and a companion came to the little cabin Muir had built near Hutchings' sawmill. Muir showed Emerson his plant collection and talked with him about nature. He took Emerson to some of Yosemite's great beauty spots.

He was disappointed when Emerson's friends, fearing for the old man's health, vetoed a camping trip he and Emerson had planned. Yet he always considered the brief time spent with Emerson among the great moments of his life.

Later Emerson wrote to Muir, urging him to come to live in Massachusetts, where, Emerson thought, Muir would find more intellectual stimulation. But Muir knew that Yosemite was now his home.

After Emerson's death, a friend found a list Emerson had made of the people he most admired. It was titled "My Men." Added at the end of the list, in Emerson's old age, was the name "John Muir." During that brief visit in Yosemite, Emerson saw that Muir was trying to live the kind of life he was describing in his writings.

Ralph Waldo Emerson, American philosopher and student of nature — including human nature.

Studying glaciers

As Muir became more widely known as an expert on Yosemite, people began to pay attention to his ideas about the formation of the valley. He continued his studies of glaciers. As he explored and examined the streaked rocks of Yosemite, he found more and more evidence that great glaciers had carved out the valleys and canyons.

Although Muir's views had solid support from much of the scientific community, some scientists scorned them. One was Josiah Whitney. Whitney was an influential scientist who headed the California State Geological Survey in the 1860s. Even though his survey had found evidence of the movement of glaciers in Yosemite, he would not accept Muir's theory that glaciers were the primary shapers of the valley. He believed that an earthquake or some sudden forceful settling within the earth had caused the valley floor to drop.

Whitney dismissed Muir as a "mere sheepherder," an "ignoramus." Whitney and his followers, who pooh-poohed Muir's theory, did not realize that in his studies of glaciers Muir was a wiser scientist than they were.

Whitney and his assistant, Clarence King, also claimed that there were no living glaciers in the Sierra Nevada. But in October of 1871, Muir found one there, and in the next two years, he would discover dozens more.

In the summer of 1872, Muir and a visitor set stakes and lines to measure the movement of glaciers. When Muir returned to the stakes on Mount McClure forty-five days later, he could see that the glacier had moved about an inch a day (2.5 cm). As James Mitchell Clarke writes in *The Life and Adventures of John Muir,* "There could no longer be any doubt that it was 'alive' — that is, neither stationary nor receding."

Facing nature's challenges

John Muir was not just a sunny-weather friend of nature. He loved nature in all its moods. More than once when he was in the mountains, blizzards approached and he found sheltered spots where he camped and enjoyed the beauty of the storms. During

"In talking to those who knew Muir, I found considerable disagreement as to which phase of natural history held first importance in his mind. One thought it was trees. Another believed it was geology. A third suggested it was plants. A fourth, probably the nearest right of all, thought it was the whole interrelationships of life, the complete, rounded picture of the mountain world. Today Muir probably would be called an ecologist."

Edwin Way Teale, in
The Wilderness World
of John Muir

A sketch from Muir's journal showing how glaciers were formed. In Yosemite many domes rise high above the valley floor.

one summer storm, he climbed high into a treetop and rode it back and forth in the gale winds, glorying in the experience.

In March of 1872 an earthquake shook Yosemite and the surrounding area. Alarmed at first, Muir was soon watching rocks crash to the valley floor and shouting, "A noble earthquake!" Meeting a group of nervous men near Hutchings' hotel, he told them not to worry, saying, "Mother Earth is only trotting us on her knee to amuse us and make us good!"

A daring mountaineer

Muir had become a true mountaineer: strong, sure-footed, and full of the courage he had shown as a boy diving into the deep water of Fountain Lake. Some may have thought Muir took foolish chances. But his almost childlike faith in the goodness of nature gave him confidence when he was in the wilderness.

In October, painter William Keith came to Yosemite with another artist and a letter of introduction from Jeanne Carr. Soon after they arrived, Muir showed the artists some beautiful Yosemite vistas and left them to sketch while he went off alone to climb Mount Ritter as he had planned.

"Never, perhaps, has there been such a complete mountaineer and glacier-climber as he, unsurpassed alike in skill, in knowledge, in passionate enjoyment."

Norman Foerster, quoted in the introduction to John Muir's Mountaineering Essays

Mount Ritter, with its summit of 13,157 feet (4,010 m), was considered inaccessible because of its steep approaches. But Muir, knowing the dangers, began the difficult ascent alone. High on the mountain he found himself clinging to a steep wall. He could see no handholds or footholds ahead, and he realized it would be almost impossible to descend the way he'd climbed. For the first time in the mountains, he was trembling with fear.

Suddenly, he felt a surge of strength and confidence, what he called his "other self." He could now see, "as through a microscope," natural footholds and handgrips in the wall, and he climbed to the top.

When his artist friends saw him returning to camp the next day, one of them later recalled that he looked like a prophet coming down from the mountain. His eyes were intensely blue. He was lean and muscular, with suntanned and weathered skin and shaggy reddish brown hair and beard. He glowed with the exaltation that mountain climbing, for all its hazards, always brought him.

Family life

In 1874 Jeanne Carr had introduced Muir to Dr. John and Mrs. Louisiana Strentzel and their daughter, Louie Wanda. Mrs. Carr thought that it was time for Muir to give up his lonely life and that Louie Strentzel

The Muir family on their front porch in 1904. From left: Wanda, Helen, Louie, and John. Although Muir sought solitary communion with the wilderness, he valued and loved his family and close friends deeply.

was a woman worthy of his great spirit. She was a college graduate and a gifted pianist. But instead of going on to the concert stage, she had stayed at home in the Alhambra Valley near Martinez, California, and helped her parents run their large fruit ranch. Muir was not yet ready for any romance beyond his love affair with nature. So it was three years before he visited the Strentzels in the Alhambra Valley.

During that time he tramped the wildernesses of California, Nevada, Utah, the Pacific Northwest and, finally, Alaska. He was awed by the tree-covered islands of Puget Sound, the majestic Olympic Mountains of Washington, the unspoiled vastness of British Columbia and Alaska. Then the solitary mountain man began to yearn for family life. He visited the Strentzels, realized that he liked this intelligent, friendly family, and found a growing attraction between himself and Louie. In 1879, they were engaged; they married in April 1880. He was forty-two; she was in her early thirties.

Louie knew she had married a man of the mountains who must sometimes leave home to explore and study. Just as he had turned to the country to escape the pressures of home and school when a child in Scotland, so he would as an adult. But from 1880 to 1888, he spent most of his time running the Strentzel fruit ranch. He was a hard worker and a tough businessman. If buyers wouldn't pay what he considered a fair price for his pears, cherries, or grapes, he would not sell. The next day they would come back and pay his price. The ranch became more profitable under his management.

In 1881, the Muirs' first daughter, Annie Wanda, was born. In 1886, Helen was born. Muir was delighted with his girls. He took them for walks, showed them the flowers, and taught them the scientific names of the plants. When they grew older the family camped in Yosemite, and the girls came to love the wilderness as he did.

But Muir did not thrive in the Alhambra Valley air. He would often miss his "real work" of studying nature and would grow thin, bothered by a cough probably caused by allergies. Seeing these signs, Louie would send him off to the wilderness.

Opposite: Yosemite Valley, with its massive rock domes and cliffs. A favorite with tourists and photographers, Yosemite National Park, in all, consists of over 760 thousand acres (307,000 ha). The National Park Service has set aside about 680 thousand of those acres as wilderness (275,000 ha).

"Brought into right relationship with the wilderness, man would see that he was not a separate entity endowed with a divine right to subdue his fellow creatures and destroy the common heritage but is rather an integral part of a harmonious whole. He would see that his appropriation of earth's resources beyond his personal needs would only bring unbalance and beget ultimate loss and poverty for all."

John Muir, quoted in S. Carl Hirsch's Guardians of Tomorrow: Pioneers in Ecology

On his trip to the Arctic in 1881, Muir sketched these pictures of three Inuit, called Eskimos *by some people: a young woman, a mother, and a hunter. Muir was impressed with the respect most native Alaskans felt for nature, but he was saddened by the corruption that white traders and hunters had brought to their lives.*

"I have camped with many men, but I have never found his equal as a man of the wilderness."

Hall Young, quoted in Linnie Marsh Wolfe's Son of the Wilderness: The Life of John Muir

Explorer in Alaska

During these years of traveling between the Alhambra Valley and the wilderness, Muir made many of his important studies of glaciers. In Alaska, he found a beautiful wilderness that contained living glaciers. With most of his studies of Yosemite glaciers completed, Muir decided to turn to the Pacific Northwest and Alaska.

On his first visit to Alaska, Muir had come to know and admire the Alaskan natives as well as the vast Alaskan shorelines. He saw the Indians' closeness to the land and water and respected their religion based on the sacredness of nature. He saw that already their culture and land were threatened by lumbering and other commercial interests. He found the vastness and rugged beauty of the Alaskan wilderness thrilling and wrote newspaper articles urging people to visit Alaska while it was still a relatively pure wilderness.

That fall Muir and a missionary friend, S. Hall Young, went exploring with Chief Toyatte and three other Indians of the Stickeen tribe to find a glacier-rimmed bay Muir had heard about from the Indians. It did not appear on any maps, but that did not worry an explorer like Muir. Their transportation was a canoe just thirty-six feet long (11 m).

Muir and Young were probably the first non-natives to see Glacier Bay and its great living glaciers. After many days of paddling, with visits to friendly Indian settlements and occasional dangers from icebergs, Muir and his group arrived in Glacier Bay. Here they discovered a vast bay surrounded by living glaciers — a landscape, as Muir would later report, still in the making. One glacier was a mile and a half across (2.4 km) and 700 feet high (210 m) at some points. It would later be named Muir Glacier.

Tracking glaciers

In the next ten years of visits to Alaska, Muir would experience a life-threatening accident and would begin writing reports that persuaded influential people to make efforts to preserve these wild areas. In 1881, Muir sailed north to the Arctic on the *Thomas Corwin*, which was on an official U.S. government search for a lost polar expedition ship. The search

was unsuccessful, but Muir was glad to visit Alaska again and see the far northern Arctic lands and seas. After his trip, he wrote reports on the botany and glaciation of the Arctic as well as newspaper articles about the Alaskan landscape. These articles began attracting many tourists to Alaska.

In a June 1890 trip back to Glacier Bay, which Muir wanted to explore, he had a brush with death. He had set up camp with a mountaineering friend. Later they were joined by a scientific party. Muir spent a few days exploring near camp before going off alone for an extended exploratory hike. He had made a wooden sled with metal runners. To the sled he lashed a sleeping bag he'd put together with a blanket and canvas shell and a bearskin lining, and his supply of tea and hardtack, a dry, flat bread like a cracker.

After several days of exploring, making detailed notes and sketches of his observations, and camping alone, Muir started back to join the main camp. Suddenly he broke through the ice and was over his head in a crevasse filled with icy water. He did not panic, as he nearly had in Fountain Lake years before, but splashed over to the side and managed to force his axe into the solid side wall of the glacier and pull

A painting of Muir Glacier by Thomas Hill. In 1879, Muir discovered this vast river of ice among the living glaciers of Glacier Bay, Alaska.

"Ever since Muir, conservationists had been praising native American peoples as wise stewards of the land. Muir admired their pantheism, supposing that — as in his own case — it demanded a respectful forbearance toward all natural phenomena. 'To the Indian mind all nature was instinct with deity,' he noted approvingly. 'A spirit was embodied in every mountain, stream, and waterfall.' "

Stephen Fox, from
John Muir and His Legacy

himself out. He moved quickly away from the crevasse, shed his wet clothes, and crawled into his bearskin-lined sleeping bag.

The night was cold and the next morning his clothes were still damp, but, like the true outdoorsman he was, he put them on and continued exploring until it was time to meet the others. He had been out alone eleven days and hiked more than forty miles (64 km). He'd lived on tea and hardtack, but the bronchitis that had bothered him for weeks before his hike was gone.

In May 1899, at age 61, Muir made his seventh and last trip to Alaska. On this trip, he made an important friend. Edward Henry Harriman, president of the Southern Pacific Railroad and one of the richest and most powerful men in America, had organized an expedition to Alaska. He invited many important scientists to come with him and his family on a combination hunting, sightseeing, and scientific voyage. Muir was to become a close friend of Harriman and his family. He also met C. Hart Merriam, chief of the U.S. Biological Survey. He hiked on Muir Glacier with some of the other passengers, including Henry Gannett, chief geographer of the U.S. Geological Survey. Years later, Gannett's research in some of the side canyons of Yosemite would confirm Muir's theories of Yosemite's glacial origins. And before long, Merriam's and Harriman's friendships would be very important in helping Muir save Yosemite Valley.

The naturalist writes

During these years, as a result of his reports and articles, Muir had been developing a reputation as a writer. In the summers of 1870 and 1871, some distinguished scientists had visited Muir in Yosemite and talked with him about his discoveries of glaciers and the role they played in forming the valley. The scientists were impressed by Muir's glacier theory and by the supporting evidence he showed them. They urged him to publish his findings. They felt that it was time to share his discoveries with a wider scientific community.

Jeanne Carr and Emerson had also encouraged him to write. Emerson wanted others to enjoy Muir's

"Of all that has been written of the scenic beauty and grandeur of the California High Sierra, the work of John Muir will live the longest, because it is close to the primeval rocks and trees that he loved so well. . . . It must be a cold . . . reader who doesn't get some thrill of that spiritual fervor which swayed Muir in the presence of the everlasting, snow-capped summits of the high Sierra."

George Hamlin Fitch, "A Tribute to John Muir: Naturalist, Writer and Man"

poetic vision of nature and read of his adventures in the wilderness. Mrs. Carr was afraid that if Muir didn't publish his findings about glaciers, someone else would write them up and take credit for them.

And once when he wrote her a glowing letter describing a snowstorm and thaw in Yosemite Valley with all the new singing waterfalls it gave birth to, she took the letter to an editor of a San Francisco monthly magazine. He liked it so well that he published it and asked Muir to send anything he wrote. Over the years Muir wrote many articles about his travels in the wilderness for that editor.

Writing was not easy for John Muir. He found it hard, slow work. As he once remarked in a letter to a friend, the work of writing, for him, went as slowly as a glacier. But his writing was gradually enabling him to raise his voice as a guardian of the wilderness.

He knew he must share his knowledge of nature with more people than he could reach merely by talking. His first published article, which appeared in the December 5, 1871, *New York Tribune*, was titled "Yosemite Glaciers." In the article, Muir carefully described the evidence he had seen that Yosemite Valley and its many side canyons had been carved by ancient glaciers.

In other articles, he wrote about the animals, trees, mountains, valleys, glaciers, and waterfalls of the Sierra Nevada and of Alaska. Believing that people would rather read a story than a factual discussion, he always wove his description and scientific lore into an exciting narrative of his adventures in the wilderness. His readers loved these dramatic, real-life stories.

Muir's fame as an authority on Yosemite grew, not only in his California neighborhood, but nationally. In the following years, Muir would have to spend more time in San Francisco and Oakland. In the city, he would be near the editors and reference books he needed to consult as he spent more time writing. He stayed with friends during the winter and worked on his articles.

Before long, Muir was earning his living by writing. He was glad to be sharing with his readers both his scientific knowledge and his enthusiasm for the beauties of the mountains.

Sketches of polar bear heads from Muir's Alaskan journal, 1881. Muir used his journals not only to write his observations but also to record them in sketches.

"Behind the heedlessly flashing axes were to be seen the sure signs of deforestation: spring floods followed by diminished stream flows, erosion, soil impoverishment, poorer crops."

Frederick Turner, in
Rediscovering America: John Muir in His Time and Ours

"Hoofed locusts" nibble grass in the Yosemite Valley, before the area was made a park and the lands were protected from overgrazing.

Land to plunder or to save

When the first European settlers came to North America, the land was covered with forests from the shores of the Atlantic Ocean to the banks of the Mississippi River. American Indians lived in those forests, cutting only those trees and killing only those animals that they needed to clothe, house, and feed themselves. They believed that all of nature was sacred and should not be thoughtlessly destroyed.

The white settlers saw the wilderness as an enemy to be conquered. Forests had to be cut down to make room for farms and towns. Wild animals were to be shot for food and in later years for sport. The native American Indians, the settlers felt, must be subdued. At first, few people spoke in defense of nature.

But by the end of the Civil War in 1865, some began to want to save the remaining forests and wild lands. In the 1870s, John Muir began to use his eloquence to teach the American people to value and protect the wilderness that remained.

As Muir traveled through the mountains and valleys of California in the 1870s and 1880s, he became disturbed at two kinds of destruction. Herds of sheep were destroying the grasses and wild plants of the meadows. And lumbermen were cutting and blasting the huge, ancient sequoia trees.

Muir was disgusted with the popular view that the land and its resources were there to plunder, that their value was only in the dollars they would bring to some sheep owner or lumberman. He wanted to save the wilderness as a precious heritage for all the people. He also knew that grasses and trees protect the land from erosion and save water. He was becoming a conservationist, an environmentalist, although those terms were still unknown to most people. As he had earlier viewed production tasks in Indianapolis, he saw that nature was one unified, interdependent system. In his writings, more and more, he called for the preservation of the wilderness.

Speaking out for nature

Muir was also asked to present lectures about his findings. At his first public lecture, in January 1876, he was so nervous that he admitted to his Sacramento audience that he was no skilled speaker and might fail them. Then he glanced at a mountain painting that his friend, William Keith, had sent to give him confidence, felt a surge of his old courage, and spoke with captivating directness and color.

Muir began to see that he would have to influence not just the general public, but also their representatives in state and national legislatures. Later that month he wrote an article related to his talk, "God's First Temples," urging the government to preserve the forests. He sent it to the *Record-Union*, in Sacramento, hoping that legislators in the state capitol there would read it and take action.

He began to work on national legislation. In the early 1880s he worked on two bills to be introduced in Congress: one that would enlarge the government-protected areas in Yosemite Valley and the nearby Mariposa Big Tree Grove, and the other that would set aside land in the southern Sierra Nevada as a public park (the area now included in Sequoia and Kings Canyon national parks).

But most people in the United States favored exploiting the wilderness rather than saving it, so it would take years of writing and lobbying by Muir and his allies before the ideas in these two bills were accepted by the public and put into law.

This postcard from 1921 shows a giant sequoia tree. The trees are as old as they are huge. Many are more than 2,000 years old. Areas where sequoias now grow, such as the Mariposa Big Tree Grove in Yosemite and the Sequoia and Kings Canyon national parks, owe their preservation in large part to Muir's efforts.

"John Muir talked even better than he wrote. His greatest influence was always upon those who were brought into personal contact with him."
Theodore Roosevelt, quoted in Stephen Fox's John Muir and His Legacy

37

Robert Underwood Johnson, Muir's editor and ally in efforts to preserve the wilderness. An influential man among literary people and congressmen and other government officials, he introduced Muir to people who could help pass laws to defend the wilderness.

A wise and generous wife

Louie Muir did all she could to help her husband in his work. In 1888, as Muir traveled through northern California, Oregon, and Washington on a trek to Mount Rainier, he became increasingly outraged at the destruction of the forests by lumberers. He wished that he had more time to fight for the preservation of the forests.

While on that trip, he received a letter from Louie. She wrote, "A ranch that needs and takes the sacrifice of a noble life, or work, ought to be flung away beyond all reach and power for harm. . . . The Alaska book and the Yosemite book, dear John, must be written, and you need to be your own self, well and strong, to make them worthy of you. There is nothing that has a right to be considered beside this except the welfare of our children."

By this time, he and Louie had earned and saved enough money that the family would be secure and comfortable for the rest of their lives. They gradually sold or leased parts of the ranch and later turned over some of the responsibility of what remained of the ranch to his sister and brother-in-law, Margaret and John Reid, and later to David Muir and his wife Juliette. This gave Muir the free time he needed to write and to raise his voice in defense of wild areas.

A partnership to save the Sierra Nevada

In 1889, Muir found a new ally in his efforts to protect the wilderness. Robert Underwood Johnson, an editor of *Century* magazine (formerly called *Scribner's Monthly*) visited San Francisco and invited Muir to meet with him. In the late 1870s, *Scribner's Monthly* had published some of Muir's articles. Two were especially popular with the magazine's readers: one on the Douglas squirrel and another, "The Humming Bird of the California Water-Falls," on a little mountain bird called the water ouzel. When Johnson had read these articles, over ten years before, he had written to Muir urging him to submit more articles. But Muir, busy with the ranch and his studies and travels, hadn't even responded to the letter. The times now were right for an alliance between these two men who both saw the urgency of protecting nature.

"Hoofed locusts"

Camping with Muir in Yosemite, Johnson listened to him lamenting the damage to the valley and uplands from the cutting of trees and the grazing of sheep, those "hoofed locusts," as Muir called them. The state of California controlled the area but was doing a poor job of protecting it.

Johnson said that Yosemite had to become a national park if it were to be preserved. He asked Muir to write two articles: one on threatened natural features of Yosemite and another on the boundaries of a possible national park. Johnson said that the *Century* would publish them, and he would use them to get support in Congress for a national park. He had some hope for success because Congress had declared Yellowstone a national park in 1872 and had set aside land in the Adirondacks as a forest preserve in 1885.

Muir wrote those articles for the *Century*, and for months Johnson traveled back and forth between his home in New York City and Washington, D.C., to lobby Congress for legislation for Yosemite. Muir also wrote and sent articles to newspapers describing the destruction he'd seen in the entire Sierra Nevada region. He wrote with vividness and passion that attracted wide public support for creation of national parks to preserve the Sierra Nevada lands. People in lumbering and sheep raising and the politicians under their influence opposed turning these lands over to federal protection. However, President Benjamin Harrison and his secretary of the interior, John Noble, supported making these lands national parks.

"His work was not sectional but for the whole people, and he was the real father of the forest reservation system of America."
Robert Underwood Johnson, quoted in Linnie Marsh Wolfe's Son of the Wilderness: The Life of John Muir

Victory for national parks

It took months, but Muir and Johnson won. In 1890 Congress passed laws creating not only Yosemite National Park but also Sequoia and General Grant national parks. (In 1940, the name of General Grant National Park was changed to Kings Canyon National Park and more land was added.) A continuing problem with Yosemite National Park was that California still controlled Yosemite Valley and would continue to until 1906.

Muir's writings strongly influenced Secretary Noble. He supported a plan for preserving large tracts

"Wilderness is a necessity. . . . Mountain parks and reservations are useful not only as fountains of timber and irrigating rivers, but as fountains of life."
John Muir, quoted in Linnie Marsh Wolfe's Son of the Wilderness: The Life of John Muir

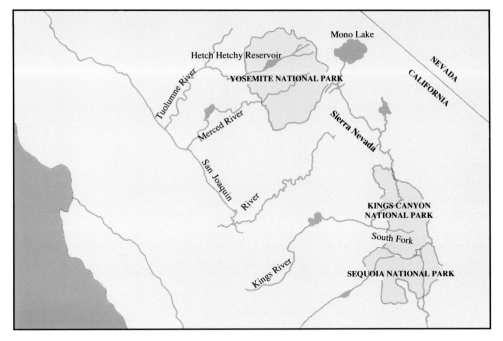

This map shows the areas that Congress set aside as national park land in 1890. People continue to lobby to add acreage to the national parks because they want to create buffer zones around the parks. These zones provide even greater protection for the animals and plants within the parks.

of wilderness. The plan, developed by Edward A. Bowers of the Department of the Interior, was drafted into a bill known as "The Enabling Act." It permitted the president to set aside as forest reservations any public lands that were "wholly or in part covered with timber." In the next fifteen years, U.S. presidents used this act to save millions of acres of forests.

But the forests were not adequately patrolled, and some ranchers continued to graze their sheep and cattle on those lands illegally. It would be several years before the government enforced its protection.

The Sierra Club

Although most Californians still favored exploitation of natural resources in the late 1800s, some saw the importance of protecting the wilderness. By 1891, a group of hikers and naturalists were ready to band together to protect the new national parks: Yosemite and Sequoia and General Grant.

Muir's friend and editor, Robert Underwood Johnson, spoke to Muir and other friends of the need for "an association for preserving California's monuments and natural wonders." Johnson saw Muir as the natural leader of such a group. Muir was shy and didn't consider himself to be a leader, but he talked to some of his friends about the idea, and they were enthusiastic.

On May 28, 1892, they founded the Sierra Club and elected Muir its president. He was to remain president of the Sierra Club for the rest of his life. He often led Sierra Club hikes in Yosemite and entertained members by telling his nature and adventure stories around the campfire.

Muir was delighted to have the support of the Sierra Club. A friend visiting the Muirs at the time of its formation later wrote that Muir came home that evening in high spirits and told his family and guest about the meeting. "I had never seen him so animated and happy before. . . . I venture to say it was the happiest day of his life. . . . Hitherto, his back to the wall, he had carried on his fight to save the wilderness. In the Sierra Club he saw the crystallization of the dreams and labor of a life-time."

One of the Sierra Club's first challenges was an attempt by a California congressman to cut the size of Yosemite National Park. Sheep and cattle ranchers were angry that their herds could no longer graze on lands that were now protected as part of the park.

John Burroughs, naturalist, writer, and biographer of Walt Whitman. This photo was taken in 1899, when Burroughs joined Muir on the Harriman Alaska expedition.

They were putting pressure on Congress. The Sierra Club, with Johnson as their contact man lobbying in Washington, protested against the bill cutting the park's size and succeeded in defeating it.

Yosemite was safe — for the time being.

The Sierra Club today

The Sierra Club's original purpose was "to explore, enjoy and render accessible the mountain regions of the Pacific Coast; to publish authentic information concerning them; to enlist the support and cooperation of the people and government in preserving the forests and other natural features of the Sierra Nevada Mountains."

Today, the Sierra Club has broadened that mission. It has gone beyond the West Coast and now works to protect the environment everywhere. Almost one hundred years after its founding, it is one of the most important environmental groups in the world. It carries on battles to save the dwindling wilderness and to reduce air pollution, acid rain, and other kinds of environmental damage as well as to educate the public on those issues. The Sierra Club is one of John Muir's great legacies.

The Nature Conservancy, a private, nonprofit organization, buys land areas that are neither large nor significant enough for the government to purchase for public use. The group protects threatened species by pinpointing selected areas for protection. Seen here is the Virginia Coast Reserve, a stretch of islands 45 miles long (72 km) that is home to 260 bird species and small mammals such as otter, mink, and red foxes.

Muir's first book

In the fall of 1893, Muir began to work on his first book, *The Mountains of California*. For the book he revised and collected many of his articles and essays that had been published separately in magazines. He received helpful editorial advice not only from his friend and editor, Johnson, but also from his wife. Louie Muir had a strong literary sense, and Muir always sought her approval before he sent off a piece of writing for publication. *The Mountains of California* was published in the fall of 1894. Muir's book was, according to one writer, "a general ecology of the Sierra Nevada," in an era before the word *ecology* was known to most people. The book was very popular and influenced many Americans to support the conservation movement.

However, many were still strongly opposed to Muir's proconservation views. Powerful lumbering and mining interests were trying all kinds of tricks to keep forest lands from becoming protected parks or reserves. These men believed they should have the right to use those lands in whatever ways would make them money. Muir and his allies knew that the forests needed better protection.

The National Forestry Commission

Some influential men joined Muir in his efforts to save the forests. Charles Sargent was the leading expert in the country on trees and forests, and director of the Arnold Arboretum at Harvard University. He and Muir became friends in 1883 and would work together on forest preservation for many years.

Sargent, Johnson, and Gifford Pinchot, a young man trained in forestry in Europe and known for his help in protecting the Adirondack forests from lumbermen, worked on a plan for saving the country's forests. In Pinchot, Muir found a compatible fellow conservationist, but they would later disagree bitterly on some conservation issues. Following the group's suggestion, in 1896 the government appointed a National Forestry Commission "to survey the timber reserves of the country, recommend the creation of new reserves, and submit a permanent policy for governing them."

"By 1890, as Muir penned his Yosemite articles and Johnson prepared for his Washington lobbying, America remained saddled with a grotesquely outmoded philosophy of public-land use characterized by cynicism, greed, and carelessness."
Frederick Turner, in Rediscovering America: John Muir in His Time and Ours

"John Muir was one of those exceptional men whose writing touches us all. The quality of Muir's vision has undeniably colored my own moods of response and clarified the statements of my camera."
Ansel Adams, Sierra Club member and renowned photographer, quoted in Stephen Fox's John Muir and His Legacy

Charles Sargent was chairman of the commission, and Pinchot was one of the other five members. Muir chose to be an adviser rather than a member.

Muir joined the National Forestry Commission in Chicago and traveled with the members on their trip to survey the forests of the West. As they traveled through South Dakota, Wyoming, Montana, Washington, and Oregon, they were dismayed by the widespread damage from lumbering and sheepherding. There was wasteful and illegal cutting and burning. Parts of the forest were blackened and leafless. Near Crater Lake in Oregon they saw "terrible desolation" of the once plentiful wild plants caused by overgrazing. In California they found that lumber groups had illegally taken over valuable forests. At the Grand Canyon in Arizona the surrounding forests were being cut and there were mines in the canyon. Many of these ravaged lands were in national forest reserves, but no one was protecting them from their destroyers.

In February 1897 the commission made its report to the president. These were its recommendations:

This photograph shows the Grand Canyon. In 1897, the National Forestry Commission advised President Grover Cleveland to make this area a national park. It was not until 1919, however, that this land was officially named a national park.

- Create thirteen new reservations distributed in eight western states.
- Change the laws on timber and mining to eliminate "fraud and robbery."
- Manage forests scientifically to maintain the nation's wood supply.
- Create two new national parks: Grand Canyon and Mount Rainier.

Congress, under pressure of the lumber, mining, and livestock lobbies, opposed the recommendations. President Cleveland, however, accepted them and used his power of executive order to put most of them into effect. The conservation forces had won this battle, but there would be more ahead.

Writing for a wider public

Muir had been writing for a rather narrow audience of persons interested in the environment. Now he was about to enlarge his audience, speaking through a number of national magazines.

For years *Century* had been the only popular magazine supporting conservation. Now the *Atlantic Monthly* asked Muir to write a series of conservation articles. Muir had been working on a book on Yosemite and, in 1895, had gone back to the valley to refresh his memory before starting the book. He had hiked through rugged canyons and up and down rough bear trails, shouting as he went to warn bears of his approach. The trip renewed his images of the magnificent area and strengthened his determination to protect it. He hoped his book would create public support for efforts to preserve the valley as part of the national park.

But the *Atlantic Monthly* was an important publication and had many influential readers. So Muir put aside his Yosemite book and an article on Alaska he was also working on and began to write the series for the *Atlantic*. The first article, "The American Forests," appeared in August 1897. He had also written "Forest Reservations and National Parks," which appeared in *Harper's Weekly* on June 5, 1897. These pieces and the others that followed played a large role in building public support for efforts to save the forests of this country.

"It was John Muir's destiny to lead men back to a realization of their origins as children of nature. 'In God's wilderness lies the hope of the world,' he said. He dared to dream of a day, and work for it, when our Government would cherish this wildness as a perpetual heritage of raw resources for all the people, and a source of healing for body and spirit. . . ."

Linnie Marsh Wolfe, in
Son of the Wilderness:
The Life of John Muir

46

His second article for the *Atlantic*, "Wild Parks and Forest Reservations of the West," appeared in the January 1898 issue. In this article, Muir described the forests as sources of renewal and refreshment for city-weary people, not just as banks of resources for the lumber industry. He recommended increasing the number and acreage of protected forest reserves. He ended the article by proposing that the forest reserves at the Grand Canyon and Mount Rainier be changed to national parks.

Perhaps his voice was heard. One year later, in 1899, Mount Rainier and its surrounding area became a national park, although it was not until 1919, under President Woodrow Wilson, that Congress established Grand Canyon National Park.

Careful readers of Muir's writing saw that he was separating himself from those people in the conservation movement, like Gifford Pinchot, who had a utilitarian view of nature.

The utilitarians believed that natural resources were to be managed for human use and profit. They did not feel these resources had intrinsic value, value in themselves rather than in their usefulness to people. They were willing to make compromises that Muir and other preservationists, those wishing to preserve nature, would not make. The utilitarians believed that we should manage forests so that we would have adequate supplies of lumber and other forest products. Unlike Muir, they did not see forests as sources of spiritual renewal and as home for wild creatures.

A split between allies

When Muir was in Seattle in the fall of 1897 on his way home from Alaska, he picked up a newspaper. There he saw Gifford Pinchot quoted as saying that sheep grazing would do little harm to the forest reserves. Muir was outraged. On the forestry commission trip, Pinchot had agreed with him that such grazing was harmful. Now he was saying what was acceptable to the sheep and cattle ranchers who had the political power in the Northwest. The break between Muir and Pinchot was part of the division between the utilitarian-conservationists and the preservationists. There would be battles ahead.

Opposite: Postcards from Yosemite National Park, 1921. Scientists and naturalists had been visiting the Yosemite since the mid-1800s. Only later in the century did tourists begin to appear in large numbers, for it had become easier to travel by rail and road.

Upper: Yosemite Village, built to house tourists and provide information and services.
Lower: Washington column and half-dome seen from the Merced River.

"The object of our forest policy is not to preserve the forests because they are beautiful or wild or the habitat of wild animals; it is to ensure a steady supply of timber for human prosperity. Every other consideration comes as secondary."
Gifford Pinchot, speaking to a meeting of the Society of American Foresters, quoted in Frederick Turner's Rediscovering America: John Muir in His Time and Ours

The endangered forests

In 1898 the U.S. Senate voted to abolish the forest reserves that President Cleveland had ordered set aside. In those days the Senate sided with powerful businesses. The House of Representatives was more in tune with public opinion, and public opinion did not support that idea. Many people were listening to John Muir's message. They were telling their representatives in Congress how important the forests were. The House defeated the proposal, one hundred votes to thirty-nine.

A new friend in the White House

Soon, a U.S. president was to seek Muir's advice. In 1901 President William McKinley was assassinated, and Vice President Theodore Roosevelt, an outdoorsman and a conservationist, became president.

He was also a reformer and was not afraid to investigate and prosecute the livestock, lumbering, and mining interests and other illegal land-grabbers who were despoiling the wilderness. Muir and other defenders of nature were happy to have an administration that would strengthen and enforce laws to protect the environment.

Roosevelt wanted to hear from informed people around the country about the problems in the forests. He had not yet met Muir, but knew he was an expert on forests. So he asked Muir's friend, C. Hart Merriam, to write to Muir, asking him to present his ideas on forest protection.

Muir responded, urging the president to follow the commission's recommendations and set up a Bureau of Forestry under the Department of Agriculture. This bureau would then be charged with protecting the forest reserves.

Four years later, in 1905, the government acted. It transferred the forest reserves from the Department of the Interior to the Bureau of Forestry (later called the Forest Service). The bureau was overseen by the Department of Agriculture. As chief forester, Gifford Pinchot headed the Forest Service and would promote his utilitarian views. Eight years later, he and Muir would find themselves fighting on different sides of environmental battles.

Fall color in the Great Smoky Mountains of North Carolina and Tennessee. The Great Smokies are the highest mountains east of the Black Hills of South Dakota and among the oldest on Earth.

The president comes to Yosemite

In 1903 Roosevelt decided to visit Yosemite. He wrote to Muir, "I do not want anyone with me but you, and I want to drop politics absolutely for four days, and just be out in the open with you."

John Muir could not miss such an opportunity to "do some forest good talking freely around the campfire," as he wrote to Charles Sargent. So he postponed a round-the-world trip he and Sargent were planning together.

A visit from the president was big news. Local and state government officials, as well as park officials, wanted to entertain the great man. They planned to keep him busy with banquets and carriage tours. But Roosevelt preferred to ride off on horseback on mountain trails and camp with Muir. The two men slept out in the open, and when they woke the first morning, they found four inches of snow (10 cm) on their blankets. "I wouldn't miss this for anything!" said Roosevelt, delighted to be in the wild with Muir.

They would talk late into the night. Muir later said to a friend, "I stuffed him pretty well regarding the timber thieves, and the destructive work of the lumbermen, and other spoilers of the forests."

"We are not building this country of ours for a day. It is to last through the ages."

Theodore Roosevelt, quoted in Stephen Fox's John Muir and His Legacy

President Theodore Roosevelt and Muir in Yosemite in 1903. Roosevelt was an enthusiastic hunter, outdoorsman, and conservationist. While Roosevelt supported efforts to save natural resources, Muir was unable to persuade him to stop the "bloody business" of hunting.

The fight to save Yosemite Valley

Muir told the president that the state of California was not fulfilling its obligation to protect Yosemite Valley from livestock and lumbering damage. He convinced Roosevelt that in order for the valley to be thoroughly safeguarded, it should become part of Yosemite National Park.

But for this to happen, the California Legislature would have to vote for re-cession, or return, of the valley to the federal government. Muir and the Sierra Club fought hard to convince California that it should return the land to the federal government. Lumbering businesses and livestock owners fought just as hard to prevent it. Across the country, many people were becoming inspired by Muir's 1901 book, *Our National Parks*, and they began vocally supporting re-cession.

The California Legislature finally voted in favor of re-cession after Muir's friend, E. H. Harriman, put the power of the Southern Pacific Railroad on the side of re-cession. Harriman supported Muir's position for two reasons: it was good environmental policy and it made practical sense. He knew preserving the valley would prove to be good business: a beautiful natural site promotes tourism, and in the early 1900s most tourists rode the Southern Pacific trains to Yosemite. Those trains employed people and brought income into the western states.

After another struggle, this time in Washington, D.C., between the pro- and anti-re-cession forces, the U.S. Congress passed a re-cession bill. On June 11, 1906, President Theodore Roosevelt signed the bill into law, and Yosemite Valley was now part of Yosemite National Park.

Muir had never liked politics. He would have preferred to be in the mountains or at home with his family, but to save the valley he had written letters, given speeches, and met with government officials in Sacramento and Washington, D.C. When the battle was over, he wrote to Robert Underwood Johnson, thanking him for his leadership and hard work to bring about this success. "I am now an experienced lobbyist," he added. "My political education . . . is finished. . . . I am almost finished myself."

*"What should Yosemite
Valley be? It should be
what it once was: the kind
of place where a person
would know himself lucky
to make one pilgrimage
there in his lifetime. A
holy place.* **Keep it like
it was."**
    *Edward Abbey, renegade
    defender of the environment,
    in* The Journey Home

*"The battle for
conservation will go on
endlessly. It is part of the
universal warfare between
right and wrong."*
    *John Muir, quoted in
    Linnie Marsh Wolfe's*
    Son of the Wilderness:
    The Life of John Muir

Family troubles

During the fight for the valley, Muir was also suffering family sorrows. In the spring of 1905, Helen had pneumonia, not for the first time. Her doctor advised dry, desert air, so Muir and Wanda took her to a ranch near Wilcox, Arizona.

While there, they received word that Louie was very sick; they hurried home, where they learned she had a tumor on her lung and would not live long. She died on August 6, after twenty-five years of marriage to Muir. After the funeral Muir and Wanda returned to Arizona to be with Helen. Muir was so grieved by the loss of his wise and generous wife that he wrote almost nothing for a year.

What finally revived his spirits was his fascination with the desert, especially Arizona's Petrified Forest. He began to learn all he could about the gorgeously colored, log-shaped rocks that had been trees over 195 million years before. He asked President Roosevelt to make this area a national monument. He hoped to save it from people who were hauling away huge pieces of petrified wood to grind up to make abrasives or to sell as souvenirs. In 1906 Roosevelt proclaimed its main portion Petrified Forest National Monument. Today the area is a national park.

Muir in the Petrified Forest, Arizona, 1905-06. Muir is examining a piece of petrified wood. The presence in the desert of these stonelike logs means that many centuries ago there was enough water in that now dry land to feed large trees.

The battle for Hetch Hetchy Valley

Muir had one more major battle in his struggle to protect the wilderness. In the 1870s, when Muir had explored the Yosemite, he had come upon a beautiful valley along the course of the Tuolumne River. The Indians called it Hetch Hetchy. At Muir's urging, it became part of Yosemite National Park when the park was established.

Thirty years later San Francisco was looking for a source of clean water and water power. Some political leaders decided that Hetch Hetchy Valley should be dammed to make a reservoir and the water should be piped to the city. They felt that providing water cheaply was more important than preserving the valley — even though Hetch Hetchy was part of a national park and even though other sources of water might be available.

John Muir was outraged: "These temple-destroyers, devotees of ravaging commercialism, seem to have a perfect contempt for Nature, and, instead of lifting their eyes to the God of the mountains, lift them to the Almighty Dollar. Dam Hetch Hetchy! As well dam for water tanks the people's cathedrals and churches, for no holier temple has ever been consecrated by the heart of man."

"How narrow we selfish, conceited creatures in our sympathies! How blind to the rights of all the rest of creation!"

John Muir, quoted in Stephen Fox's John Muir and His Legacy

This cartoon, titled "Sweeping Back the Flood," appeared in the San Francisco Call. *It makes fun of Muir and others for fighting a losing battle in opposing the damming of Hetch Hetchy.*

A view of the verdant Hetch Hetchy Valley, on the Tuolumne River, before it was dammed.

"'The Eternal events pile up,' John Muir used to say as he contemplated the course of human history. Disturb the balance in nature's economy or in society, and you reap droughts, floods, wars, class struggles, revolutions. These will continue until man shall have learned the universal law of cooperation."

Linnie Marsh Wolfe, in
Son of the Wilderness:
The Life of John Muir

Conservationists against utilitarians

The struggle over Hetch Hetchy went on for years. It caused many fights in the conservation movement, even in the Sierra Club. Many of the San Francisco members believed the Hetch Hetchy dam was necessary. Muir and his supporters, however, fought long and hard over this period to try to convince Congress, various presidents, and secretaries of the Department of the Interior to save the valley.

The fight got mean and dirty. Supporters of damming Hetch Hetchy tried to discredit Muir and his allies. One San Francisco politician even accused Muir of having cut trees in Yosemite just as the lumber companies did. This was not true. When Muir had worked as a sawyer for J. M. Hutchings in 1869 he had sawed only fallen timber. More than 100 great pine trees had fallen in a windstorm and Muir sawed only those trees.

Gifford Pinchot, favoring utility over preservation, was still chief forester and led the fight in Washington for the dam. Several times Muir thought that the valley would be saved. But in 1913, under President Woodrow Wilson, Congress voted to give the city of San Francisco permission to flood

Hetch Hetchy Valley. That beautiful valley was forever lost. The purpose of the national parks — to preserve scenic places — had been violated. And, ironically, San Francisco could have gotten water from other sources at no more expense.

Defeat

This was a major defeat for Muir. He had written letters, pamphlets, and articles; given speeches; held meetings; and worried about Hetch Hetchy for years. Near the end of the fight, he wrote to Helen, "I'll be relieved when it's settled, for it's killing me."

This was not the last time that the need of cities for water conflicted with efforts to preserve wilderness areas. Sometimes opponents compromised. Other times the supporters of dams won. But in 1954, when the U.S. Bureau of Reclamation wanted to flood a wild mountainous area called Echo Park, close to Dinosaur National Monument in northwestern Colorado, the preservationists fought hard.

They showed legislators and officials pictures of the beautiful Hetch Hetchy Valley as it looked before it was flooded. Then they showed what it looked like after flooding, with its muddy banks and exposed tree stumps. Senator Hubert Humphrey of Minnesota spoke against the Echo Park Dam in the Senate. He said, "You have only to look at the picture of Hetch Hetchy today to see how wrong were the prophets of 1913." Finally Echo Park was saved.

Gifford Pinchot, who headed the U.S. Forest Service, was once an ally of Muir. A utilitarian, he later split with the preservationists on conservation issues.

More traveling, more writing

During the years of the Hetch Hetchy struggle, Muir had also been doing other writing. In 1911, he published *My First Summer in the Sierra* and, in 1912, *The Yosemite*, a guidebook to the region. Muir's friend, E. H. Harriman, loved the stories that Muir told and wanted him to write an autobiography. Muir resisted the idea. When he was visiting the Harrimans at Klamath Lake, Oregon, Harriman assigned his secretary to follow Muir around and take dictation as Muir told him his stories. Muir later revised the typescript from this rambling conversation into *The Story of My Boyhood and Youth*, which was published in 1913. In 1912, he began again to sort

"We are in a fever of almost hysterical emphasis on science as a material weapon. . . . Our civilization needs to adopt the mountaineer pace, somewhat slower, but steady and upward."
Olaus Murie, director of the Wilderness Society, 1945-47, quoted in Stephen Fox's John Muir and His Legacy

through the material in his Alaska journals for another book. He worked on this book until the end of his life.

In those years Muir still had the urge to explore, to see more of the natural wonders of the world. In 1903, after President Theodore Roosevelt left Yosemite, Muir joined his friend, Charles Sargent, for their postponed trip around the world. He was away from home for more than a year. Museums and palaces bored him, and he found himself homesick and worried about his family so far away, but he loved the forests and broad plains of Russia, the forests of Australia, the great peaks of the Himalayas.

At last, in 1911, Muir set off on the trip he had planned to South America in 1867, when he had hiked to Florida. This time he took a ship out of New York. In Brazil he sailed up the Amazon River into the jungle. He also traveled to a remote ridge on the western slope of the Andes where he found a grove of monkey-puzzle trees he'd been searching for.

In December he sailed from Montevideo, Uruguay, to Africa. Again, he had come to visit the trees he'd heard of but never seen. Near Victoria Falls, he wrote Helen, he found the great baobab trees with their "skin-like bark and . . . massive trunk and branches. . . . The Falls too are grand and novel. . . . Smoke-like spray ever ascending, watering the woods with constant showers."

Last years

In his last years, he was saddened by the deaths of several good friends. He had worried about Helen's health, but now she was well and married. She, her husband, and three sons lived in the Mojave Desert near Daggett, California. Wanda was also married and lived on the Alhambra Valley ranch with her husband and four sons. Just as he'd enjoyed his girls when they were young, Muir enjoyed his grandsons. During this period, he often took trips to visit friends — people and trees and mountains. He continued to work on his Alaska book, reliving the great sights and adventures of his travels there. But in the late fall of 1914, his chronic cough seemed worse. He told Wanda that he wanted to go down to Daggett to see Helen and her husband and children.

While he was there he weakened and died of pneumonia on Christmas Eve, 1914. On the table beside his bed was his Alaska manuscript.

John Muir's continuing influence

Muir's influence did not end with his death. A friend finished typing and editing Muir's Alaska notes, and another friend wrote an introduction. *Travels in Alaska* was published in 1915. In the years since his death many of his essays, letters, and journals have been published, with new collections and editions appearing regularly. His voice is still raised in defense of the wilderness.

His accomplishments are still with us. Every year millions of Americans come close to the wilderness in our national parks. In fact, the crowds visiting Yosemite are so large that private cars are now barred from some parts of the valley. Like Yosemite, the Grand Canyon, Mount Rainier, and Petrified Forest national parks all became protected by the government at Muir's urging. Some historians call him the "father of our national parks."

The conservation movement has grown, and preservationists like Muir have increased in numbers and power. Due largely to the work of conservation groups, millions of acres of wilderness are protected today under the United States Wilderness Act of 1964. Local, national, and international groups continue working to protect our lakes, forests, farmland, and cities from threats like acid rain.

Besides the still influential Sierra Club, the Wilderness Society, Defenders of Wildlife, Nature Conservancy, and many other organizations fight to preserve the forests and other wild places. Colleges and universities teach courses in ecology and environmental studies. Such courses teach students about the interconnections that Muir observed and valued over a hundred years ago.

Ongoing conflict

Yet there are still struggles between those who care about protecting nature and those who want to exploit and let future generations worry about repairing it. Even within the conservation movement, utilitarians

Greenpeace members use nonviolent direct action to stop those who are polluting the Earth. These activists are calling attention to a company that is dumping toxic waste directly into sewers where it cannot be treated to remove harmful elements.

Once we could venture off our planet and see its wholeness from space, we understood more clearly that it was our home, that we must be stewards of the Earth.

"When we try to pick out anything by itself, we find it hitched to everything else in the universe . . . . The whole wilderness in unity and interrelation is alive and familiar. . . . the very stones seem talkative, sympathetic, brotherly. . . . No particle is ever wasted or worn out but eternally flowing from use to use."

John Muir, quoted in Linnie Marsh Wolfe's Son of the Wilderness: The Life of John Muir

battle preservationists. The utilitarians try to balance progress and profit with the need to protect the environment. The preservationists put protection of nature above other values. If Muir were alive today, he would surely be among the preservationists.

We know which side he would take in the controversy about opening the Alaska wilderness to more exploring and drilling for oil. The vast destruction caused by the oil spill in Prince William Sound in the spring of 1989 shows how dangerous to the environment transporting oil can be. We see how carelessness in government and industry can affect the lives of fish, birds, and sea mammals; how it can foul beaches and islands; how it can ruin the livelihood of people.

We know how Muir would hate the stockpiles of nuclear weapons and the tons of toxic waste that threaten all life on our planet. We know how he would deplore the reckless cutting of tropical forests and the pressures to cut more and more trees in the national forests of the Pacific Northwest.

Fortunately there are people today who understand, as Muir did, that all life is interrelated. That our air, our water, our food depend on how well we care for our Earth. That the wilderness can teach us and comfort us. We must hope that their message reaches into the hearts of those who have not heard.

Many hard decisions lie ahead. How can we feed billions of people without using dangerous pesticides? How can we meet the need of cities, industries, and farms for water without losing valleys and canyons? How can we supply the paper and lumber that our civilization requires without destroying the forests that protect our atmosphere and shelter so many species? How can we mine ores and fuels without destroying land? Some answers may come from technology. But technology is not enough. We must change our attitude about ourselves and our world. We must learn from dedicated people like John Muir to respect the Earth and to protect it.

Lands designated by the U.S. government as part of the National Park System, the National Wilderness Preservation System, and the National Wildlife Refuge System, as of 1988. The blue dots indicate National Park System lands, the pink dots indicate National Wildlife Refuge System lands, and the purple dots indicate National Wilderness Preservation System lands.

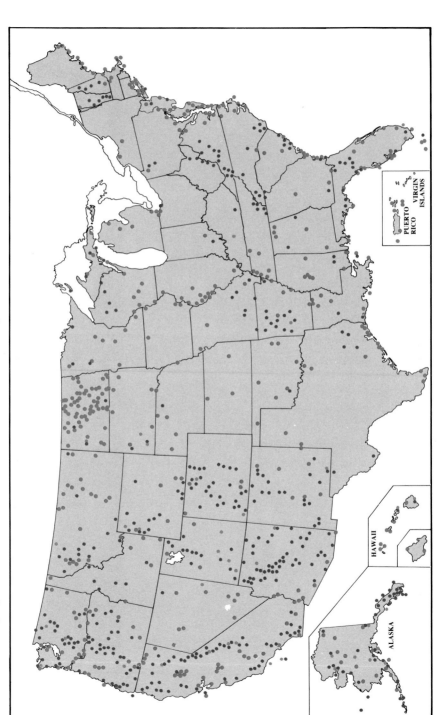

60

Lands set aside for the U.S. National Park System

Listed below are the approximate numbers of acres set aside, by state and territory, as national parks. Many of these parks are part of both wildlife refuge areas and wilderness preservation regions.

Alaska	41,450,198		Nevada	76,800
Arizona	1,311,907		New Mexico	46,755
Arkansas	5,824		North Dakota	70,416
California	2,089,398		Oregon	160,290
Colorado	317,278			
			South Dakota	271,594
District of Columbia	6,466			
			Tennessee	520,270
Florida	1,571,784		Texas	851,536
Hawaii	263,482		Utah	835,239
Kentucky	52,370		Virgin Islands	14,696
Louisiana	20,000		Virginia	195,072
Maine	42,252		Washington	1,669,947
Michigan	571,790		Wyoming	2,530,340
Minnesota	217,892			
Montana	1,013,595			

Total acreage set aside as parkland in National Park System	56,177,191
Total acreage in National Wilderness Preservation System	89,033,462
Total acreage set aside in refuges and ranges in National Wildlife Refuge System	88,598,425

Source of information: Sierra Club. For more information write to the Sierra Club at the address listed on page 62.

For More Information . . .

Organizations

Listed below are some organizations that work to protect the environment. Some publish newsletters or magazines. They may also have member groups in your area that provide speakers. Write to the organizations listed below for more information about the subject of interest to you. Tell them clearly what you want to know, and give your name, address, and age. Your community may also have a nature center where you can get information or take part in educational or conservation programs.

Canadian Parks and Wilderness Society
Suite 1150, 160 Bloor Street East
Toronto, Ontario
Canada M4W 1B9

Defenders of Wildlife
1244 19th Street NW
Washington, DC 20036

Environmental Defense Fund
257 Park Avenue, South
New York, NY 10010

Greenpeace USA
1436 U Street NW
Washington, DC 20009

(For information on national parks only)
National Park Service
Department of the Interior
P.O. Box 37127
Washington, DC 20013

National Wildlife Federation
1400 16th Street NW
Washington, DC 20036

Sierra Club
730 Polk Street
San Francisco, CA 94109

Wilderness Society
1400 Eye Street NW
Washington, DC 20005

World Wildlife Fund — Canada
60 St. Clair Avenue East, Suite 201
Toronto, Ontario
Canada M4T 1N5

World Wildlife Fund — U.S.
1250 24th Street NW
Washington, DC 20037

Yosemite Association
P.O. Box 545
Yosemite National Park, CA 95389

Books

The following books will tell you more about John Muir and the land and animals he loved. Some will tell you about the national parks, the conservation movement, and other people who have worked to save the wilderness and protect our world. The first four books will enable you to share in Muir's experiences as he describes them.

By John Muir —

My First Summer in the Sierra. (Houghton Mifflin)
Stickeen. (Heyday Books)
The Story of My Boyhood and Youth. (Berg)
Travels in Alaska. (Houghton Mifflin)

About John Muir —

From the Eagle's Wing: A Biography of John Muir. Swift (Morrow)
John Muir: Father of Our National Parks. Norman (Messner)
Muir of the Mountains. Douglas (Houghton Mifflin)
Trails of His Own: The Story of John Muir and His Fight to Save Our National Parks.
    Grossman and Beardwood (Longmans, Green)

About Nature and Naturalists —

All About Mountains and Mountaineering. White (Random House)
Ecology: Science of Survival. Pringle (Macmillan)
Glaciers: Nature's Frozen Rivers. Nixon and Nixon (Dodd, Mead)
Great American Naturalists. Coates (Lerner)
Guardians of Tomorrow: Pioneers in Ecology. Hirsch (Viking)
Heroes of Conservation. Squire (Fleet)
*Man's Mark on the Land: The Changing Environment from the Stone Age to the Age of
    Smog, Sewage, and Tar on Your Feet.* Gregor (Scribners)
Naturalist-Explorers. Blassingame (Franklin Watts)
Pioneers of Ecology. Cox (Hammond)
The Story of Geology: Our Changing Earth Through the Ages. Wyckoff (Golden Press)
Trees Alive. Riedman (Lothrop, Lee & Shepard)

Glossary

botanize
    To study plants on outdoor field trips or to collect plants to study later. (See **botany**.)

botany
    The study of plants. Botany is a branch of biology, the science of life in all its forms.

conservation
    Using resources wisely, not wastefully. The conservation movement supports
    creating and protecting national parks and forests. But some people in the movement
    have been willing to see controlled lumbering, mining, and development
    in wilderness areas. (*See also* **preservation**.)

ecology
    The science that examines the relationships among living things and elements of their
    environment. The term, *oekologie* in German, was coined by a German scientist
    named Ernst Heinrich Haeckel in 1869. Although Muir did not use the word *ecology*
    in his writings, his work shows that he was intensely aware of ecological principles
    and interrelationships.

geology
    The science of the history of the Earth, especially as it is shown in rocks. Often
    rocks give evidence of glaciers, earthquakes, or floods that occurred many
    thousands or even millions of years ago. But geologists do more than simply look at
    samples of stones. They study great landforms like mountains, canyons, and
    plateaus, as well as geological features of the seas.

glaciation
The forming of glaciers or the effects produced by the movement of glaciers. By examining the marks on rocks, scientists can tell if a glacier passed over them. Muir discovered evidence that Yosemite Valley was carved by a series of glaciers.

glacier
A slow-moving sheet of ice that carries with it rocks and other debris as it scrapes the earth. During the Ice Age many thousands of years ago, glaciers covered much of North America and parts of Europe and northern Asia. Active glaciers still exist on high mountains and in parts of Alaska and other far northern lands.

moraine
A mound or hill formed by earth and rocks that were carried by a glacier.

national monument
An area set aside by the government to preserve an interesting natural feature or historic site for the public.

national park
An area of special scenic value set aside by a government for people to enjoy and study. National parks usually are larger and provide more sites for camping and recreation than national monuments. Some areas originally set aside as national monuments later became national parks — for example, the Grand Canyon and the Petrified Forest. In the United States, the National Park Service also controls and protects national seashores, rivers, lakeshores, and other areas for the public.

naturalist
A person who studies nature. The title *naturalist* is applied more accurately to a biologist working out in the field than to one working in a laboratory.

ouzel
A water thrush. John Muir describes the ouzel as a "joyous and lovable little fellow, about the size of a robin, clad in a plain waterproof suit of bluish gray, with a tinge of chocolate on the head and shoulders . . . the hummingbird of blooming waters, loving rocky ripple slopes and sheets of foam as a bee loves flowers, as a lark loves sunshine and meadows." He found water ouzels near every waterfall in Yosemite.

Petrified Forest
An area, now a national park, where there are large, beautifully colored logs that over millions of years turned to stone. The park includes Blue Mesa and part of the Painted Desert. John Muir studied the Petrified Forest in his old age.

plant press
A clamping device for flattening and preserving plant samples for later study.

preservation
Keeping a species or area from harm or extinction. Preservationists emphasize protecting natural resources rather than using them. (*See also* **conservation**.)

sequoia (*Sequoia sempervirens*)
A variety of large redwood tree growing along the coast of northern California. A grove of this variety, located near San Francisco, has been named Muir Woods.

sequoia (*Sequoiadendron giganteum*)
> Another kind of redwood, huge trees found in Yosemite, Sequoia, and Kings Canyon national parks. Some are three thousand years old. John Muir fought against lumbering these beautiful, ancient trees.

sierra
> *Sierra* means *saw* in Spanish; a range of mountains with a jagged profile like the cutting edge of a saw is called a sierra.

Sierra Nevada
> A large range of mountains extending along much of the eastern part of California. It is so bright, with its snow-covered summits, that Muir calls it the "Range of Light."

Chronology

1838   **April 21** — John Muir is born to Daniel and Ann Gilrye Muir, in Dunbar, Scotland.

1849   Muir's family leaves Scotland. Many flee hard times in Europe hoping to find riches in the California gold rush or in the fertile lands of the United States. Daniel Muir joins a religious sect in the United States.

1857   The Muirs move from Fountain Lake farm to Hickory Hill farm nearby.

1860   John Muir leaves home, takes his inventions to the Wisconsin State Fair in Madison, and works briefly in Prairie du Chien. He becomes close to Jeanne and Ezra Carr. Abraham Lincoln is elected president.

1861   Muir returns to Madison and the University of Wisconsin. The U.S. Civil War begins.

1862   Muir works as a grade-school teacher while still at the university, continues inventing, and studies botany and geology.

1864   Muir leaves Wisconsin for Canada, explores woods and marshes, and works in a sawmill and broom and rake factory near Meaford, Ontario, with brother Daniel. Lincoln signs bill giving Yosemite Valley and Mariposa Big Tree Grove to California as state park lands.

1865   Civil War ends.

1866   Muir returns to United States. He works in a carriage-parts factory in Indianapolis, where he develops labor-saving procedures.

1867   **March** — Muir is temporarily blinded in factory accident; when his vision returns, he decides to leave factory work and study nature.
September 1 — Leaves Indianapolis to begin his "Thousand Mile Walk."

1868   **January** — Muir leaves Florida for Cuba.
February —He sails for New York, then via Panama to California.
April — Arrives at Yosemite. Keeps daily diary of his nature observations.

1869   **June** — Herding sheep for Pat Delaney in high pastures, Muir explores mountains and valleys, and finds evidence of glaciers.

1870	Muir winters in Yosemite Valley and works at James M. Hutchings' sawmill. **April** — He begins guiding tours of Yosemite.
1871	**May** — Ralph Waldo Emerson visits Yosemite and spends time with Muir. **December 5** — *New York Tribune* publishes Muir's first article, titled "Yosemite Glaciers."
1872	Scientists disagree on Muir's theory on glaciation of Yosemite Valley; Muir gains fame as authority on Yosemite and guide to its treasures.
1873	Muir stays in Oakland; he begins writing articles on Yosemite.
1874	San Francisco's *Overland Monthly* starts publishing Muir's series, Studies in the Sierra. Muir returns to Yosemite, travels north, and climbs Mount Shasta.
1875	Muir moves to San Francisco and writes for five years, with many visits to the wilderness. He is outraged by the lumbering of California's giant sequoias.
1876	**January 25** — Muir gives first lecture, to Literary Institute of Sacramento. **February 5** — *Sacramento Record-Union* publishes his article, "God's First Temples," urging government preservation of the forests.
1877	Muir travels widely in mountains, forests, and valleys in Utah and California; he continues writing and lecturing.
1878	*Scribner's Monthly* publishes Muir's "The Humming Bird of the California Water Falls"; Muir begins corresponding with the Strentzel family.
1879	Muir becomes engaged to Louie Wanda Strentzel; he makes his first trip to Pacific Northwest and Alaska.
1880	**April 14** — Muir and Louie Strentzel marry. **July 31** — Muir goes to Alaska again.
1881	**March 25** — Annie Wanda Muir is born. **May 4** — Muir sails on the *Thomas Corwin* to Arctic on search for lost polar expedition ship. Muir spends most of the next seven years running the Strentzel-Muir fruit farm; he suffers from poor health.
1884	Muir takes Louie to Yosemite.
1885	Daniel Muir, Sr., dies.
1886	**January 23** — Muir's second daughter, Helen, is born.
1887	Muir begins work on *Picturesque California*.
1888	Visiting Mount Shasta and Mount Rainier, Muir is outraged by damage.
1889	Muir meets Robert Underwood Johnson, who persuades Muir to write articles urging protection of Yosemite Valley and pledges to support effort.
1890	Muir's articles published in *Century*; Muir visits Alaska again; Yosemite and Sequoia national parks established; Yosemite Valley is still under control of California.

1892	Muir and others form the Sierra Club.
1893	Johnson introduces Muir to many literary, scientific, and business leaders in New York and New England; Muir travels to Scotland and Europe.
1894	Muir publishes his first book, *The Mountains of California*.
1896	**June** — Ann Gilrye Muir dies. **July** — Muir accompanies U.S. Forestry Commission on its survey of forests.
1897	**February** — Forestry Commission reports to President Grover Cleveland. **June 5** — Muir's "Forest Reservations and National Parks" published in *Harper's Weekly*. **August** — Muir's "The American Forests" appears in *Atlantic Monthly*. Both articles create popular support for preserving forests.
1898	Muir lobbies in Washington, D.C., for conservation.
1899	Muir travels to Alaska with Harriman Expedition. Mt. Rainier National Park established.
1901	Theodore Roosevelt becomes president; he supports conservation.
1903	**May** — Roosevelt tours and camps in Yosemite with Muir; Muir leaves on round-the-world trip with Charles Sargent.
1905	**May** — Muir and Wanda take Helen to Arizona to recover from pneumonia. **August 6** — Louie Strentzel Muir dies.
1906	**June 11** — Yosemite Valley becomes part of Yosemite National Park. Muir studies Arizona's Petrified Forest; Roosevelt later proclaims the area a national monument.
1908	Roosevelt proclaims Grand Canyon and Muir Woods national monuments. Preservationists begin fight to prevent flooding of Hetch Hetchy Valley.
1911	Muir sets sail for South America and Africa; he reaches Africa in early 1912. Muir publishes *My First Summer in the Sierra*.
1913	Congress votes to allow use of Hetch Hetchy Valley as a reservoir. Muir publishes *The Story of My Boyhood and Youth*.
1914	**December 24** — Muir dies of pneumonia.
1915	Muir's *Travels in Alaska* is published.
1916	National Park Service established to protect and manage U.S. national parks.

Index